"The strength of a family, like the strength of an army, lies in its loyalty to each other."
— Mario Puzo

What Are My Parents Doing All-Day?

"A Childish Way to Explain Adulting"

When I go to school, I wonder what my parents do?

Are they superheroes?

When It's Bedtime, what do my parents do?

Do they stay up all night and have fun without me?

Why are my parents so mean if I don't listen?

>|<
x x

Why do my parents always say no at the store when I want something?

They keep saying money doesn't grow on trees...I don't believe them.

Oh children.... We will do our best to answer your exciting questions.

When you go to school, we go to work. We work hard each and every day to earn money for the home we live in, the food we all eat, and to make sure you kids have everything you need for school. That way when you become adults you will be prepared.

Are we superheroes? In our own family, we just may be.

When it's bedtime, mommy and daddy reconnect from the long day. We tell each other about our workdays, communicate tomorrow's plan as a team, and finally our favorite part is sharing our favorite memories of you kids from the day....

Most certainly not a party.

After all of that, we get ready for bed just like you, so we wake up with energy to do it all over again with you!

Why do we act mean sometimes?

We don't try to, everything we do and everything we plan has a time limit, which means the quicker you listen, the more time we have together for activities.

Why do we say no often at the stores when you kids want something?

Well, we work each day to make money to afford our home, our food, and the ability to keep us all clean and clothed. Money does not grow on trees; it's earned from hard work and commitment. As much as we would like to, we can't buy everything we want otherwise we can't afford the important things we need for our family. Nothing you kids need to worry about.

That's what mommy and daddy do when we are not with you.

It's all for you.

The End